Seasoned Poetry
Poetry by the Seasoned Poets
of the Blue Ridge

Tenth Anthology 2013

Acknowledgements

Elda Lepak is grateful to the editors of the following publications in which some of her poems first appeared: *Wisconsin Poets' Calendar 2012, Main Street Rag, Sky Canvas*

First Edition 2013
Printed in the United States by Createspace

Format and Cover Design: Elda Lepak
Photography: Elda Lepak, Laurabeth "Rusty" Breeding
Editors: Helen Palmer, Gwyneth Noble

ISBN -13   978-1482592986

This anthology

is dedicated to

E. Eugene Noble

and

HB Russell,

honoring the memory

of two good men

who were great admirers

of the Seasoned Poets of the Blue Ridge.

Foreword

Seasoned Poetry—a title that promises the spiciness of aging without the staleness of having been left too long on the shelf. It suggests the thoughtful musings of poets who have seen many seasons.

This tenth offering by the Seasoned Poets of the Blue Ridge ranges from poems inspired by the re-visiting of poets Dickinson and Millay to the observations of the change of seasons in the Blue Ridge in Hendersonville, North Carolina. In the nineteen years our group has met weekly, our lives and our poetry have been tested by the changes and losses wrought by the seasons of the year and of life.

Current Seasoned Poets of the Blue Ridge

Laurabeth "Rusty" Breeding
Karen Heggen
Elda Lepak
Elizabeth B. Martinez
Gwyneth Owens Noble
Helen Palmer
Beverly Bryan Russell

Table of Contents

Helen Palmer

As a very "seasoned" poet, I seek to find fresh ways to capture the sights and convey the emotions of the changing seasons. The fickleness of February, annoyance at all the debris of late winter, awe at the kaleidoscopic beauty of our flowerbed in June, and the versatility of the Bradford pear, with its early white flowering and its late fiery display—all have been subjects of my pen's admiration.

Even as the natural world elicits poems, the advances of technology seem to echo the threats of advancing years; old age meets the iPhone and the Nook. I still write my poems on a yellow pad; they just get polished and printed on a laptop computer.

"Intimations of mortality" continue to infuse my poetry, especially after surgery to remove an ovarian cyst in 2011. I rejoice at the possibilities of each day.

Reality Check

Suggestions of spring...
Birds on the wing...
Greeted by song...
What could go wrong?

Daffodils emerge...
My spirits surge...
Winter's dirty snow
promises to go.

February's fickle.
Remember, winter's sickle
cuts many a bloom
emerging too soon.

Thoughts upon Blowing the Driveway

Spring beauty
has its negatives,
like the thorns on a rose
or the dirty dishes after a feast.

For every cluster of petals
on a dogwood tree or weeping cherry,
the spent blooms clutter
lawns and skylights.

As maple leaves burgeon,
their whirlybird seeds
rain down and later
the worm-like, stringy flowers
create nests that
blow across driveways.

The pines drop
their dried needles
and drive us crazy
with sneeze-producing
yellow pollen
coating cars and
window sills.

How can we complain
when all this mess
is designed to assure
that spring beauty
will return next year?

God's Flower—Dianthus

Of all the flowers of spring in bloom right now
the shy dianthus sheds a weakened glow,
her perky flowers and crenellated brow
outdone by rhododendron's powerful show.

And if she needed more to make her shrink,
next to her, well named, a knockout rose does thrive--
a shock of pink, so vibrant one would think
a painting of Monet had come alive.

This common flower, a favorite of mine,
adds color to baptisia's green and blue.
She nestles next to nodding columbine
and waits for peonies' pink and rose debut.

She tells me that, in any floral view,
the wallflowers also have a job to do.

Still Autumn

Middle of November--
red splotches in a dreary landscape--
leaf piles now mulch,
brown oak leaves still pestering us...

But Bradford pear trees dazzle
with their show of crimson leaves
tipped with green...

Infrequent parades of such trees,
planted in rows some twenty years ago
before we knew
how fragile the branches during ice or snow storms...

Today we cherish these surviving
non-fruit bearing pears--
in early spring their blossoms as refreshing
as vanilla ice cream cones,
in late fall their colorful leaves
as luscious as caramel apples.

Intervention, Anyone?

Computer games--
solitaire, bridge--
have stolen my time,
wrecked my dreams.

I slide from e-mail
to Hoyle for just a "while,"
find that I have wasted
two hours stacking
virtual cards
and bidding
imaginary hands.

Even worse,
like Frost
in "After Apple Picking,"
I play solitaire
in my dreams,
shut my eyes
and move the cards around.

What is the appeal
of these mindless games?
Simply that they
allow me to escape
the world and its worries.
Cheaper than a pill,
but, still, unsettling.

Charging

My mind is in a daze
as gadgets proliferate.
I worry with all the ways
to keep them up to date.

With laptop, cell, and Nook
recharging is required.
How long? Must I look?
The questions make me tired.

Back in the good old days
with power outlets or land lines,
phone, TV, and library book
needed no pampering time.

Just as I start the crossword
or have a cat in my lap,
I am driven to check my email
and update the latest app.

I'm ruled by these devices.
They cost money and time.
Retreating is not an option.
Just let me whine in rhyme.

On Being Retired for Twenty-three Years

When I consider how my days are spent:
walking the dog and tending to the cat,
cleaning a house and chasing annoying lint,
eating Ann's cooking and avoiding the fat,

I remember the days when I faced the youth.
I shepherded them in their student days,
hoped that they'd learn to seek the truth.
I was steeped in teenagers' yo-yo ways.

My attention's now on politics and obits.
My friends all walk with replacement parts.
My fingers are stiff with crippling arthritis.
Reaching my toes is among the lost arts.

Though I complain about age in this sonnet,
I seek no stone with my name etched on it.

Face the Facts

It's easy to invent a life.
Just fill out forms on line.
Create a Facebook page with pix
of you at twenty-nine.

Invent a birthplace, career highs,
fiancé and wedding date.
Invent some offspring--bright, of course--
and brag about your mate.

It's harder to escape the truth,
not to wonder if you've mattered.
What have you done with all those years?
Were you just treading water?

Trier, Germany

Bicyclists, backpackers, tourists
from bus and riverboat tours
pour into Trier. Encircling
the guide with the yellow flag,
they stand expressionless,
tied to the whisper gadgets
in their ears. They move
en masse from one ancient monument
to another. Awed by the Roman Basilica,
they miss the quirky knitted bootie
some wag has tugged on to the bare
stone foot of a cherub on a garden statue.

They march past cathedrals and
remains of Roman walls
looking for the W.C.
and the Euro Shop
on the first floor
of Karl Marx's birthplace.

Quilted Northern

I love to travel, see the world,
try new foods, new flags unfurled.
I love the accents, ancient sites,
the chance to know of others' plights.

Yet on return I sigh with pleasure
as I enjoy TP's soft texture.
No more of that waxed paper wrinkle
whenever I am moved to tinkle.

I know that I should give more thought
to all the waste flushed down the pot.
Europeans learned to save the planet.
The earth's resources have a limit.

American Idyll

They rest in the late summer pasture,
half lying on a carpet of browns and greens,
a couple of daisies near their bare feet--

two boys feeding on the leisure
of a summer day,
hat brims pulled down,
knickers billowing around their slim shanks.

The two gaze into the distance,
away from the easel and brush of the artist

seeming to relish this moment
away from chores and schoolbooks.

In our day they would be fiddling
with smart phones or
listening through buds of iPods,
wearing baseball caps backwards
with jeans hanging from their hips.

They would never see
the dolphin-shaped cloud
in the sea
of the sky.

Form--*ekphrasis*: A written description of a work of art.
Boys in a Pasture by Winslow Homer, 1871

A Life

Down Time's quaint stream
a rivulet
descending from the mountain
cascading over ancient rocks
diverted by debris
trunks of trees
felled by the axe of age
or the gnawing of greedy teeth

on past the dams of commerce
under the bridges high and low

until it reaches
a deep pool
a rest
before it joins
the eternal seas

First line from Emily Dickinson

Perspective

So many years
       of greeting autumn,
so many years
       of leaf ho-hum

till this year
       with a wake-up call
I thought I'd not
       be here next fall.

Now as the mountain
       turns to gold
I remind myself
       this view to hold,

and now I count
       the painted leaves
and thank the Lord
       for my reprieve.

Gwyneth Owens Noble

This past year I have faced many passages. The biggest of all was my dear husband's death. I am making every effort to regain balance. Some of these poems illuminate challenges I have faced along the way.

I have passed silently
from the young old
to the old old,
a position embraced
by my husband
years ago, but one
I have valiantly fought.
It was the most painless
painful transition
I have ever made.
So painless in fact
that I didn't recognize it
until it had happened.

Lifetime Learning

I want to take a class
on being old.
I want to accept indignities
as they unfold.
I want to learn to stand up straight again.
I want to run.
A class could teach me to accept my fate again
before life's done.
There may be so many more skills
that I can learn to do.
If not, I want a graceful way
to accept that, too.
I want to learn these things
before life has expired.
I've always been a faithful scholar.
Now I'm only tired.

Handle With Care

I am feeling frail,
an old fashioned word.
I never felt this way before.
I fell.
And I did not break.
That should make me feel strong.
On the contrary.
It has reinforced my feeling
of fragility.
I want to be popped
into a box
full of popcorn
marked *Fragile*
Handle With Care
and be mailed
To Whom It May Concern
Contents May Break
Do Not Bend or Crush.

Auld Lang Syne

He wears old jeans he still calls overalls,
a warm sweater, slippers worn down at the heels.
With hair pinned unattractively behind my ears,
I say, ruefully, *I would call someone tonight*
but they're all dead.

The New Year's Eve Party.
Not with regular friends but New Year's Eve Friends,
once a year friends,
an unusual group, all alumni of a small college.
Newly married that first party sixty years ago
they celebrated the freedom to drink openly,
embrace others from a safe marital place.
Dot, our first hostess, crawled under the coats
piled on the bed in their compact apartment
and went to sleep halfway through the celebration.
Gone, now. Her husband, too.

The next year our first son slept under the coats
at Barb and Walt's. Barb monitored whose turn it was
to host the party, but died early, leaving us in a muddle
when Walt's second wife declined to join the revelry.
Dee and Pete were a disappointment
moving to another social orbit, perhaps in embarrassment
after opening her sparkling burgundy that exploded,
drenching the newly hung wallpaper
in the kitchen of our tiny, proudly-owned home.
Sam and Bunny, Mary Lou and Ray, mainstays for years,
moved away, drifted out of our lives. Others came and went.

In later years raucous parties became stately sit down dinners.
Yet certain traditions were sacrosanct.
Charades, the kisses at midnight, your husband always first,
my yearly cigarette, a ritual urged on and applauded
by the heavily smoking crowd.
The teary struggle through Auld Lang Syne.
Each year promised endless possibilities.

This year at nine, carrying his pre-dinner martini,
he gives me a kiss and shuffles down the hall to bed.
The music plays on, Vienna celebrates.
The ghosts keep dancing.
Possibilities are finite.

I push my husband

in his wheelchair
to the small gazebo
set in the manicured lawn
of the Rehab Center.
We question another similar building
looming to our left,
invade the serenity of a young man
working on a laptop, who smiles politely,
folds up his work and leaves.
A sweating laborer
uses a noisy trimmer nearby.
I am teaching my husband
to use an iPod
full of the music from his CD collection,
laboriously and lovingly assembled
by a friend. We settle the ear buds.
For old fingers and minds confused
by the latest technology
the operating mechanics are not intuitive.
There is no on/off button, no volume control.
Menu has taken on a new meaning.
The silver button in the middle
has no identification.
One must slide, not press.
We achieve only a modest success
but a smile creases his face.
How could we know
that in two weeks
he would be in the building next door?
The Hospice.

Not Yet

A week after my husband's death
I venture out alone.
The check-out clerk greets me
with a hearty
How are you today?
I don't know how I am
so I mumble, *OK.*
She keeps the conversation going,
How about that rain last night?
Did it rain last night?
I don't know.
Withdrawing from her attempt
to engage me I blurt out,
My husband died last week.
Immediately
a great hush comes over her
and the people behind me
look away.
I have unfairly involved them somehow
in my grief.
I'm so sorry, she says.
Thank you.

Unwilling tears come.
As she bags my groceries
I sense her swallowing
her usual rejoinder,
Have a great day!

Maybe I'm not ready to shop.

Transitions

It is terrifying
to be summarily dismissed
from your job
after sixty one years
of loyal and loving service.
It's true
I had been given notice.
It was evident the position
was close to ending.
A larger effort
on my part
brought diminishing results.
There were no complaints
from my employer
that I wasn't doing the job well,
never an inkling of dissatisfaction.
Thank yous and kind words
filled my days.
Others felt
I was in denial,
was no longer able
to meet the demands of the job.
At my age
retraining seems ridiculous.
I sit
on the back porch
staring into space,
knowing the emptiness
and despair
of the unemployed.

Messages

My husband always kept
the bird feeders full...
until he couldn't.
While his mobility lessened
his concerns for his birds
grew.

I was enjoined
to carry the feeders
to the garage
where he would sit
on a rickety chair
and fill them up.
I would replace them
in the garden.

Today
a persistent cardinal
hops up and down
on the empty feeder,
chirping noisily.
I like to think
it is a messenger
from my dear husband
reminding me
of my job.

Puh tee kee ee

In hot pursuit of staying young
there's one device I've always clung
to, learning words pristine and new
so I could smartly add them to
my vocabulary.
I found a new one yesterday,
it inadvertently came my way.
The doctor hemmed and hawed, then said,

It's not unusual, all that red,
It's called petechiae.
There's really nothing you can do.
Your foot is red. It's not the shoe.
Relax, in time it too might fade
but what addition you have made
to your vocabulary.
It's really age that brings it on.
The capillaries sing their song
and make themselves appear so brightly
and if you still were young and sprightly,
you'd never learn that word!

So now I'm left to ponder if
this word I've added to my list
is one I *really* want to know.
I doubt it, but if that is so
it puts me in another class
called *really* old. I think I'll pass.

Dreaming

It's always hard to face the truth
in ripe old age or fresh, chaste youth.
I know my footsteps aren't as sure.
I find my thought not always pure
but faced with tasks both large and small
I still think I can do it all.
I see myself as long ago
and hope the ravages of time don't show.
An idle wish to which I'll drink
but anyhow
that's how I think.

I'm traveling to a distant place
moving with customary grace,
an aide appears with this broadside
with just one look at flagging stride,
not caring for my damaged pride
and with a smile she does confide,
I'll get you a wheelchair.

Between the Bookends

My father seemed to slip easily
into 20th Century life.
Leaving a tiny village in Wales
he settled with his wife, his mother,
and two small girls, soon joined by another,
in a busy industrial city in Ohio.
The adjustment seemed effortless
as he spent most of his life
in books. Books were his stability,
his comfort, his companions, his joy.
Today is his birthday.
He's gone, of course.
He would be one hundred and fourteen,
born in the dying days
of the century that produced
Darwin, Chopin, Dickens, Queen Victoria.
How ancient that seems!
I have already kissed
the 20th Century, my century, goodbye,
but I'm still floating there,
loathe to embrace the easy technology
second nature to my grandchildren.
Like my father I, too, hug my books,
spurn the embrace of Kindles and Nooks,
rail against automated, disembodied voices,
the social networking
that captivates this generation.

My adjustment is uneasy.
Will my books have the power
to save me, too?

I'll Tend to This Later

When a large stack of papers piles up by the phone
and begins to careen to the floor
it attracts my attention, rivets my mind
with the knowledge I have to do more
in bringing some order to this hapless mess.
A separation process begins:
here are bills to be paid, letters to write,
lists, that grow lists, to weigh in.
The check book and calendar enter the fray
as I sort obligations from fun.
Which charities this month command my largess,
which ones all my patience have run?
The denouement is dismal for this oft-told fable.
I've moved all the mess to the dining room table.

If My Dog Could Talk

she would spin 1001 tales,
become the Scheherazade of dogdom.
A thrice-rejected graduate of a municipal shelter
she came with this admonition,
She hates cats and babies.
Having neither, we signed on.
But what has she loved?
This lady of mystery tells nothing.
Does she cling to the memory of those
who taught her to sit, stay and shake?
As her little paws wrap around me
in loving embrace
is she remembering other loves?
With the imperiousness of a true princess
she creates a throne on the master's chair,
rearranges a nest of pillows on the mistress' bed.
There is no humility here.
A smile from me sets her tail wagging.
When I come home she circles the house
wild with joy, then begs to go out.
Am I not the one she's been waiting for?
Catlike, knowing the value of work,
she lurks under the bird feeder,
not stalking birds but the vole
tunneling below, harvesting seeds
falling providentially from above.

Diana, the huntress, pounces.
In the cold, dark of a winter night
she ignores my calls, is loathe to come in
to the warm comfort of her bed.
Is she in communion with woodland sprites,
gathering new stories, searching for new loves?

Come in, I beg. Forget your past.
I want to be your only story.

Poetry readings and meetings

Elda Lepak

Out of my soup kettle of dreams and memories, I ladle poems, taste them, add seasonings as needed. A teaspoon of basil here, a pinch of thyme there. The mood of each poem is as different as the spices selected–soothing, dramatic, or with just a hint of mystery. I keep working on the recipes. My goal is to satisfy my hunger— to create poems so that no two taste exactly alike.

Determination

I remember
watching ants,
being impressed
with their ability
to carry crumbs
twice their size.

It must have felt
like the weight
of the world
and yet they
persisted,
day after day,

like new parents.

Would I Be the Me I Am?

We were identical Aquarian twins
born with peach fuzz hair.
Our names were derived from our
Finnish grandmothers,
      Elda from Edla
      Evelyn from Eveliina.
For years I wanted to be Jennifer,
so smooth, so sophisticated.
I considered being Evelyn but cosmically
thought it unfair, perhaps unwise.
Evelyn died at thirteen days.

I think of her (us) and the other twins
who went through elementary
and high school with me.
Their lives read like the *Bobbsey Twins.*
They were popular, pretty,
and in their younger years, dressed alike.

Hand-me-downs don't come in twos.
One child at a time was all this family
could manage.
Smart girl. Evelyn knew
love was already stretched,
patience had its limits.
She looked around, chose to escape,
try again for a more welcoming family.
She left me with memories I never had.

Transient Beauty

Just over night the Bradford pear trees
turned white with spring blossoms.
Millions of delicate patterned petals
cling to bobbing bare branches.
The trees boast pear-shaped crowns,
their namesake,
even though they don't bear fruit.

I drive with no destination in mind,
past fields, forests, and village yards,
admire each tall, fragile tree in turn.
One majestic tree after another trumpets
the start of spring.

I sigh at the first hint of lime green leaves
that follow the blossoms,
push their way open,
overpower the shuddering blossoms
forced to fall like the last snow of spring.

Summer Storm Sequence

A crescendo of thunder
rolls along with graying clouds
playing bumper pool across the sky.
Lightning, like a fractured arrow, flashes
towards earth, lands with a deafening snap.

Rain follows as if someone unzipped the heavens.
Wind chases the deluge sideways
until it hits the house with the force of a pressure hose.
The skies relax, tired after their dramatic display.
Clouds drop a steady patter of rain,
empty the last of their loads.

The grass shivers in relief, stretches tall.
Flowers raise their faces, shake off the muddy dust,
and sponge up the needed moisture.
Birds emerge from their tree branch shelters,
swoop through the lingering drops.
They sing, anticipate the feast of surfacing worms.

The sun finds a hole and punches through,
making rooftops glisten.
Trees dazzle with iridescent glitter.
The cooling air smells fresh, like line-dried sheets.
One last soft rumble of thunder rolls off
the distant drifting clouds.

The Farmer's Lot

The newly planted clearing lies in wait
for him to come and tend to tender roots,
to pull the weeds and water tiny shoots.
The morning sun shines down upon the plot
and gives its blessing to the farmer's lot.

Although he does not dare believe in fate
he fears the dangers of excessive rain
and bugs or wilt or sun and drought--
each can negate the hoped for, fought-for gain.

It's hard, this life of living off the soil,
weeks and months and years of endless toil.
As crops are gathered through each season
the farmer finds no simple way or reason
to explain his love for all he helps create.

Endings

In autumn I wander the wrinkled hills,
enjoy the leaves, colored and bent,
falling and fallen around me.

With each step I hear them crunch,
hear the whisper of soggy grass,
and feel twigs snap beneath my feet.

Fall has a distinctive smell,
a blend of brisk harvest air
spiced with the passing of summer.

This turn of season finds me sifting
through a year of change,
a year's worth of memories.

I associate fall with endings.
My sad endings are put to rest
with the fallen leaves on wrinkled hills.

Little Books of Happiness

The newspapers are full of
back-to-school specials
but I have yet to find one ad
for really cheap spiral notebooks.

Each fall I buy several books
even though I am not taking classes
and have no school children.
There is something compelling
about the bright covers of red,
purple, pink, yellow, and green,
all filled with blank pages
with narrow blue lines.

To open a new, clean notebook
is like opening a new chapter of life,
full of anticipation and expectation.

Welcome Home

Learning a new house takes time —

the high pitched whir of the dishwasher,
the squeaking board in the hall,
the right position of the shower dial
to make the temperature yours.

It takes two months to remember
which light switch works which light,
that the door lock must be turned
just as the door is shut so it can catch.

It takes the turn of seasons
to learn how to get heat, not cold air,
to decide where the Christmas tree belongs,
and find out if ten boxes of decorations fit —
somewhere.

It takes a year to change the wall paint,
pull the rug that now seems ugly,
and to find wanted unpacked items.
Another year and you forget
what hides in the attic boxes.

Then you go on a trip,
return to the house,
and realize you are home.

Found Pennies

A copper penny
bright as the hot sun
caught my attention.
I picked it up,
saw the 1962 mint date.
It aged well
for being fifty years old.

Attending my fifty year
high school reunion,
I found that few friends
had kept their shine.
The accumulation of years,
bad choices, and heredity
dulled their appearance.

Discussions flowed
like spring streams
running fast,
bouncing over obstacles.
Old personalities emerged,
memories created smiles,
and caught my attention
like that old penny.

Abandoned

An iron fence entwined with ivy
and knotted weeds surrounds the property.
An elaborate gate lies flat in the long grass,
pasted into the earth by composting leaves.

A once-white mansion crouches
behind massive oak trees.
Limbs as large as grown men reach out, flex,
poised either to protect or pierce the roof.

Inside, papered walls wilt, ceilings droop,
and spiral staircases waste away.
Beyond the back door, boxwood hedges
outline the garden, overpower it, dwarf the space.

Centered is Artemis, Goddess of the Hunt,
coated with grime, trimmed with green moss.
Her bow is missing, her arrows broken.
She gazes in anger upon the present,
weeps for the past.

Danica Remembers

At Christmas time you came to Florida
and we stayed in a villa that had
lots of rooms and a pool.
We played mermaids and ship wreck.
Grandpa was a shark and swam after us.
Inside, we pretended the bunk beds were a fort.
You told me stories and I acted like
all the people.   We played with my
Barbies and Bratz dolls, and had restaurants.
One night we were eating cake in the kitchen
when the lights went out in a storm.
Grandpa put a flashlight in a glass
and the light went up to the ceiling.
Our faces were glowing
like in candle light.
The room was full of shadows
changing shapes.
You and Grandpa had coffee,
I had milk. That was fun.
Do you remember, Grandma?

In North Carolina we pedaled a boat
way into the lake.
I threw corn and bread crumbs
to noisy ducks and geese that
followed us.
It was a parade
and we were the front float.
Later we had a picnic and
the geese wanted my sandwich.
Do you remember, Grandma?

We were at Uncle Alan's wedding
in Arizona when I was little.
It was outside at a golf course.
I wore a fancy dress
and threw red petals on the grass.
After the wedding I picked them up
and did it a bunch more times.
We stayed in a condo then.
Grandpa and I walked to a playground.
I was ahead and told him
there was a good haircut.
I meant short cut.
We laughed.
Do you remember, Grandma?

When we moved into our new house in Florida
you came to visit us.
I wanted to show you the park and pool.
You said not to run so fast,
you wanted to see me.
You didn't want to get lost
and I know you can't run any more.
I know you are old.
That's okay.
I love you, Grandma.

Consider the Period

The keyboard characters
called an election to delete
the smallest of members.
They deemed the period
too minuscule
to carry a place on the board.

The Punctuation Party prevailed
upon the voters to pause,
ponder the point.
Most sentences do not include
all twenty-six letters of the alphabet,
but the majority of sentences
do end with a precisely placed
period.

Karen Heggen

Season of the Long View

As October leaves begin to fall
bright, cool sun sweetens the view
of early autumn's brilliant days.

Then clocks turn back to shorter days.
November comes when leaf fall
opens the season of the long view.

Dusk's long shadows bring into view
the contrasts of these shorter days.
Moods move, too, through rise and fall.

Fall days can change our point of view.

Though the weatherman called 2012 a warm winter here, two hospitalizations and an extended recovery led me to other adjectives. In April 2012 our poets led a four-week class at Blue Ridge College. *Remembrance* is a sonnet from that celebration of Emily Dickinson and Edna St. Vincent Millay. *When Winter Comes* was written in the summer of 2012 as loss laid bare the lives of friends. *Season of the Long View* was written as an exercise in the tritina form. It became healing to consider memories of childhood and recent events, to allow humor and gain a longer perspective. May poems such as *Lee Fruit, Great Blue Heron*, and *Maru* offer you a warming gift and open your own memories.

When Winter Comes

When winter comes
laurel leaves curl
against the onslaught
of drying winds
and too bright sun
on melting snow.

When winter comes
growth continues
underground.
Roots gather strength
to feed spring buds.

When winter comes
quiet colors fill the woods.
Not all is gray
if one looks closely.

Some see bright
bittersweet berries.
Some see nandina.
Others see holly.
Some celebrate
burled branches,
peeling bark,
moss and lichen,
evergreen boughs overlooked
in warmer seasons.

Watch for signs
of subtle beauty
when winter comes.

What the Camera Didn't Catch

Snow photos take note of January days
when the camera lens reached outdoors
but the photographer didn't.
Views out the window remain
in memory at month's end.
Enjoy them here by words alone:

The pair of hawks that soared,
then sat sunning their tawny breasts
on a high bare branch nearby.

The first footprints along the driveway
were made in eight inches of snow
by a white bulldog with caramel colored
blotches on her back, caramel colored ears
above a silver-studded pink collar.

She walked along the roadway just above the curb.
When I whistled she came bounding up the driveway,
let me chuck her under the chin, made several circles
in the snow before making tracks north toward
the unknown home from which she had roamed.

As the snow began to melt around the plowed roadway
the mockingbird took up its accustomed flight
across the side street across the five-lane,
landing behind plow-formed mini-mountains,

leaving me with anticipation
of seeing more clearly
what holds his interest,
once the snow mountains melt.

Through the Rearview Mirror

Objects are closer than they appear.
So says the passenger's side mirror.
Eyes dart from traffic ahead
to landmarks along the way,
a look in the mirror to see
what is coming up on one side,
to see the scenery now passed,
to see who is riding on your tail.

Stopped in a lakeside park
with a new camera, she takes
a notion to frame a shot
of an infant in a stroller,
beside his skipping sister
and smiling parents, seen
within the confines
of the driver's side mirror.

Another shot shows the peopled
pavilion along the shore, complete
freedom to catch candid views
of children at play, adults
laying out the day's picnic.

Face to face may be a view
too close for some insights.
Check the rearview mirror.
Find what is going on now
in those places where you've been.

To Understand a Smile

To understand a smile
remember it is a gift given
and a gift received.

See how a smile carries
a torch that can light a room.

A smile may lead to laughter.
or to tears. It s not a smirk.
A smile is kind.

A smile may bubble up
from deep springs,
quench many a thirst.

It costs little, yet
may be valued much.

Watch it spread and grow
from eyes to lips, to face,
to form, from being to being,
from soul to soul.

To understand a smile
remember one
you have shared.
Feel your body relax,
your heart open.

Orange Crush

That 1950s summer at Memorial Park,
a block above the diving dock,
the Washburn, Wisconsin town kids
drank what they called *pop,* glass bottled,
pulled for them from the lead-lined,
cold-water cabinet at the concession stand.

I was odd-girl-out because to *my*
St. Louis-raised *city mind*, those bottled
fizzy drinks were called *soda*. To *them*
soda stood solely for the work of a Soda Jerk,
a concoction of ice-cream, flavored syrup,
and hand-pulled seltzer water served with
a long-handled spoon and a straw in a tall,
footed glass at the main street malt shop.

Just thirteen that Orange Crush summer,
I was still unembarrassed by my orange tongue
and the matching ring around my mouth
that Orange Crush would leave.

My cousin Joyce, a year older, was *careful*
in what *she* drank, known to include
the grown-up taste of grapefruit-flavored Squirt,
as she laughed her way through the orange *crush*
she had all summer on Teddy,
the copper-haired boy
who operated the concession stand.

Lee Fruit

A cross between
a tangerine and a grapefruit.
It is Thanksgiving week as she thinks
of the connection between the holiday season,
the thin-skinned Lee fruit, and her mother –
now a dozen years gone.

How many years since she first stood
at the Farmer's Market and asked the produce vendor
what would be easy for her elderly parents to peel,
what would have few seeds with which to deal?
Lee Fruit was the answer.

Thus began the years when Lee Fruit
was carried some seven hundred miles
to brighten holidays.

Memory leads her to look for Lee Fruit *this* year.
Finding none in town, she heads out some twenty miles
to the place where she first found them.
They are larger this year.

She buys a bag, not the big box
of those early years. The skin is thin, easily peeled.
The flesh is a juicy combination of sweet and tart,
a subtle difference from tangerine and orange.

She sends some to her sister
for her November birthday,
reminds her of the history
that flavors each bite.

The Beach at Sainte-Adresse

At the shoreline, rest three beached dinghies.
The foremost, bright deep blue with yellow oars.
The sky, full of gray daubs of density,
dark to light, full of chill, consumes
nearly one-third of the canvas.
Left foreground, inland, three men
stand behind two more beached boats.
Blue jacket, blue cap, a pipe-smoker converses
with a fellow whose sweater is as gray
as the beach. The third wears a jacket
the color of the darker boats, dark blue-gray.
He leans forward, out of the conversation,
eyes on the graveled ground.

Three sailboats glide across the quiet bay,
their red-gray sails stand in contrast
to the brighter blue-green water.
The nearest boat bears three sails.
A seated painter at water's edge
directs his attention toward those sails.
The shoreline sweeps in a semi-circle,
encompassing the town. Humane and timeless
are the nearest buildings. Until, at the end of the long spit
that borders the far side of the bay, the scanning eye
sees smoke stacks of advancing industry.

Groups of three objects echo throughout.
An artist's expression of balance.
Intended or unintended intimations
of yesterday, today, and tomorrow…

Form—*ekphrasis:* A written description of a work of art.
The Beach at Sainte-Adresse, by Claude Monet, 1867

Consequences

Words resound inside my head,
rhythms trip and tumble, jangle, jumble.
Passion, pity, pain, pleasure, pressure
or remorse, each rumbles in their course.

It is an art, the turn of phrase, the turn of gaze
upon the past, upon the present close at hand,
upon distant lands and times, in keeping with
the stand the mind finds tempting in its tumbling.

Yet, I think of one whose turnings are in wood:
at first rough-chunked, gradually understood
by hand and lathe. Listening for its Muse
to whisper what it will become as it surrenders
to the willing mind, the shaping hand.
Mentors flash their fluency before his eyes,
boldly balanced, barefoot, astride the cutter's tool:
lathe, wood, artist's body one.

Another works in clay; mixing, rolling, turning,
shaping on the wheel, willing to be cold and wet,
to let fly the power to strike out, and stretch on,
and then to set to fire the shape when deemed as done.
Then celebrate the shape and heft when cleft from fire,
before first glaze renders an amazing difference.
Single-toned or studded with enticing variety of ornament.
Some glow. Some show hard shine, high polish bouncing
approaching light. Some crazed, their character rendered
in fault lines checkered on the surface. Others, subtly sanded,
draw the eye inward: suggest earthier aspirations.
Skilled artist's rendering of what once
was unintended consequence.

Groundwater

Have you walked in the woods
or across an untended field
and found your foot unexpectedly
put upon spongy ground, ground
which makes a soft sound underfoot,
ground which may show lichen or
leaf litter as your eye takes in
the imprint you have made
and makes you think of hidden
springs bubbling up from
an unseen source…

The field of memory
holds such wonders.

What meaning to draw, what
refreshment, what thirst abated
when on your daily rounds
you hear the sound of a certain song
or at the store you see a redhead
of a certain tone, a certain curl,
a certain way the person walks.
Memory bubbles up.

Groundwater, from a deep,
hidden source, refreshes
today's field of being
with the filtered water
of yesterdays' rains
and long ago
waterfalls.

Great Blue Heron

On a January morning
after a grating glitch in
a new electronic wonder

     after paying a tax bill
     and giving thanks
     for wind-free sunshine

I drove along
Four Seasons Boulevard,
beside the swamp

     where a wingéd blue giant
     arose over the highway before me --
     the uplift

        sufficient to soothe
        the other challenges
        the day would offer

Remembrance

If in the years to come you should recall
these hours of sharing Dickinson and Millay,
perhaps your mind will focus after all
upon a face, a line of grace, a play
on words which elevates your present mood…
a thrill of spring, a scent, a sunlit day
when you knew poetry would do you good.
So, read aloud a favorite poem, the way
Vincent might have raised her voice and stood
before a friend or audience unmet,
or to herself, as one who might have read
a letter from Emily, with regret
that you were not face to face, and yet
feel lifted. *These poets are not dead.*

First line from an Edna St. Vincent Millay sonnet.

Written for a class about Emily Dickinson and Edna
St.Vincent Millay given by the Seasoned Poets at
the Blue Ridge Community College.

Maru

Big screen to small screen.
Movies in theaters to movies on TV
to videos on TV to videos on your computer
or your cell phone.
I am enchanted by a cat, Maru,
born in 2007, born in Japan.
His female owner has made videos
of Maru since he was a teenager.
The most you will see of Maru's human
is her hand, and that not often.

Such an exuberant cat. Such a clever owner
to introduce him to boxes and bags
big and small that he can explore,
that he can attack, that he can wear.

Such an invention, YouTube,
that allows people all over the world to
become charmed by Maru by the millions.
My introduction was by email
from a friend a hundred miles away.
Maru makes me smile, reminds me
of the days when my cats were young.

Reminds me of the days when I was young.
Those days it would have taken
weeks to hear from a foreign pen pal
about her amusing pet whose name
meant *round*, who lived half a world away.

A Thousand Thursdays*

Hyperbole
to say a thousand days.
Who keeps count?

It is not the quantity, but the quality of days,
the output of lines that comes to mind,
that cheers the heart, that reawakens desire.

Yet think of your own life.
How parts of it were ordered
by certain days, days important
though unnumbered.

School days, club days, church days,
lunch days, music days, sports days,
letter days, TV days, play days, work days,
pay days, anniversary days, holidays,
bill pay days, days made up of scheduled hours…

Wakeup hour, lunch hour, dinner hour,
travel hours, homework hours, housework
hours, reading hours, visiting hours, practice
hours, pet hours, puzzle hours, prayer hours,
social hours, private hours, quiet hours.

A thousand days, a thousand hours
come and gone. We may not number them.
But do take count of them. The patterns
of a lifetime become us as certainly as
the splendid moments of serendipity
we choose to remember.

*Our Seasoned Poets Group has met each Thursday for almost two decades.

Laurabeth "Rusty" Breeding

"Rusty" having Christmas fun with her hiking buddies

The Seasoned Poets of the Blue Ridge have been writing together for over eighteen years. My poem, **No Laughing Matter** makes a humorous comment on being "seasoned." The poem **Something to Do** reminds us of endless possibilities. Although we always start with a **Blank Page**, **To Catch a Poem** gives some advice on how to start. There's more timing advice in **One Last Trip to the Kitchen**. **Taking Flight**, **The Rainbow** and **Trapping the Bug** take us into the summer season, as does the word painting of Norman Rockwell's **The Runaway**. There is a little nostalgia in **Kitty's Gone**, but **Moving On** is an attitude that will carry us into more exciting seasons to come.

To Catch a Poem

Poems come from who knows where,
who knows from what direction.
Wish that they would fill the air
and wait for a selection.

Perhaps the weather is the cause
or something someone said.
Sometimes one settles if you pause,
sometimes while you speed ahead.

They seem to show up when they please,
but it's an even bet
a poem will drift in on a breeze.
Be ready with a net.

Taking Flight

How can I think *poetic*
with so many things to pack?
Days have become frenetic,
so many details to track.

Three weeks the bag has lain open,
more items squeezed in every day.
I haven't flown since who knows when.
New rules have come into play.

Into checked luggage or overhead bin,
goes the Zip-Lock of medications?
As I study instructions again and again
I recall my old-time vacations.

Be careful what metal I put in my purse;
it's disclosed in security's pan,
along with my shoes and here is what's worse –
I may be tapped for a body scan.

Valid passport and drivers' license,
they'll accept for identification.
Though screenings seem not to make any sense,
they require my compliant cooperation.

Sweaters and swimsuit in the bag to be checked.
Record an account of what's in it.
Four seasons of weather I'd better expect.
Just remember the forty-pound limit.

The Rainbow

Red, orange, yellow,
green, blue, violet.
Every band of the spectrum
dazzles
in a low-slung arch
across the highway.
Ends drop into puddles of golden mist
that slide along the pastures
as we drive.

On-coming cars emerge under it.
Passing traffic splashes through it.
We can never catch up to it.
But I'll swear I spy
that pot of gold at the end.

Something To Do

As my neighbor and I
wave "Goodbye"
after our morning walk,
our talk, our fun,
we say to each other,
"Remember how Mother
often reminded,
'It's time to go home
and get something done!'"

There was always work
to be done on the farm
where each of us,
as children, knew
in spite of all the country charm,
there was never an end
to something to do.

No need now to enumerate,
even try to abbreviate,
a list as long as
a country mile.

The lesson learned:
rewards are earned,
brings back the memory
and our smile.

Trapping the Bug

To the ceiling clung a little brown moth.
I could have let the creature be.
Not the sort that eats holes in cloth,
it was bothering nothing, no one but me.

A plan, a strategy, method or art
had to be delicate, quick, precise.
Success be apparent right from the start.
Opportunity seldom happens twice.

Balance on ladder or the bedroom chair.
One hand holds a pint-size glass.
Press to the ceiling, trap the insect there.
Dislodge with a careful thin-card pass.

The card becomes the glass's lid.
Carry your prize out the nearest door.
Release the moth just as I did.
But wait, there's more, there's more.

Back into the house that brown moth fluttered!
You don't know when you're lucky! I muttered.

Kitty's Gone

The kitty's gone; new owner found.
I didn't know I had felt so bound.
Unaware of how it rankles
to have a kitty round my ankles.

Doors are open; I feel so free
to have the whole house just for me.
No more kitty litter scattered –
Kitty didn't think it mattered.

No more scampers chasing ball
or somersaulting down the hall.
No more attacking paper bag
or lunging at a dangling rag.

No more climbing up the bookshelf,
with volumes tumbling on herself.
You learned porch-rail walking past the gate.
Sorry, kitty, it's too late.

So quiet now for Number 1
without little tabby having fun.
I'll sit a bit, perhaps a nap,
but miss that kitty on my lap.

Runaway (1958) *Norman Rockwell*

The burly, pistol-packin' cop on the barstool
is the first to capture attention,
but the ankle-to-ankle posture
of his black jackboots on the foot rail
and the sensitive tilt of his shoulders
toward the child betray a softie.

The boy could be eight years old.
His yellow T-shirt, jacket on his lap
and dangling shoelace catch our eye.
He listens intently to the officer.

A coffee pot sits on the counter;
a pie rack against the wall
and a 1940's radio on its shelf
are details that don't distract us
from the 3-way conversation:
policeman, cook and boy.

At the foot of the boy's stool
lies the key to the scenario:
a bundle of belongings wrapped
in a red kerchief, secured
on a shoulder-ready stick.

We know it's guy-talk.
The cook could be saying,
I tried that once when I was a kid.
Didn't work out too well.

The cop could be saying,
I'm gonna get you into
our kids and cops club.
The boy's demeanor says,
I'm think I'm going to be
a policeman when I grow up.

Form--*ekphrasis*: A written description of a work of art.
Runaway by Norman Rockwell 1958

Words

Sometimes words are poetry
Sometimes words beguile
Sometimes barked in authority
Sometimes voiceless in a smile

Words are used for explanation
Words can calm and words can rile
Words may need some concentration
Words by nature, versatile

Words can find a million uses
Only words can make excuses

To Understand a Fraction

(It's all gobbledy-gook to me)

To understand a fraction
     you have to understand halves
     and not-halves. Do not confuse
     not-halves with have-nots.

To understand a fraction
     you have to understand wholes
     and not-wholes. No,
     not-wholes are not knot-holes

To understand a fraction
     you have to understand quarters.
     Quarters can be divided by roommates.
     Drink machines take multiple quarters.

To understand a fraction
     cut a quarter in two
     and you have eighths.
     The past of eats is ate, not ates.

To understand a fraction
     demonstrate with a pie.
     Do not confuse a circular pie
     with *pi* in a circle.

To understand *pi* in a circle
     is tomorrow's lesson.

No Laughing Matter

Again the conversation turns to pills,
our aches and pains and corresponding ills.
When we were young it seemed a running joke
at the expense of older folk –
how Grandma Jane and Grandpa Bill
were slave and servant to the ever present pill.

But time and tide have turned and thus
the older generation now is us.
Health and vigor which we took for granted
to our amazement's been supplanted.
The topics, now, that we discuss
are anything but humorous.

One Last Trip to the Kitchen

Is there a bumper sticker that says,
One Last Trip to the Kitchen?
We could use a reminder.

Bread dough I meant to chill – left rising.
An hour from home I remembered,
could see it mushrooming out of the pan.

Last minute phone call, email update,
list *to take*, list *to get*, locks to lock, taps to close,
appliances to unplug, burners to check.

Is this the *brain freeze* they're talking about,
the deluge of information,
the details that overload our culture?

How many catastrophes caught,
how many tragedies prevented
by one last trip to the kitchen?

Moving On

I'm tired of thinking 'bout the past	1
and the future's not that long	2
there isn't time to feel downcast	3
let's brew our coffee strong.	4
And the future's not that long	2
no sense in counting days	5
let's brew our coffee strong	4
mock the dull malaise.	6
No sense in counting days	5
enjoy things as they come	7
mock the dull malaise	6
be a bit adventuresome.	8
Enjoy things as they come	7
take a different point of view	9
be a bit adventuresome	8
so much in the world is new.	10
Take a different point of view	9
there isn't time to be downcast	3
so much in the world is new	10
I'm tired of thinking 'bout the past.	1

pantoum: A verse form composed of quatrains
in which the lines have the pattern shown above.

Beverly Bryan Russell

Poems come from all the directions of my life experience: happiness, nostalgia, love, anger, awe, sorrow. I must capture them quickly because they are elusive when I see them from the corner of my eye.

I hope these words speak to you, touch you. Maybe you will find yourself in them.

Strangers in the Night

I love to walk the night woods with my dog.
One winter evening we walk outside.
I take my flashlight.
She lifts her nose, races up the hill,
announces her barking presence.
I fear bears, skunks, whatever.
Curiosity makes me climb the path.
The black dog is grinning proudly
and looking back to the ancient beech tree
where a suet feeder is nailed.
The intruder is an albino flying squirrel
now scrabbling in fright.
We apologize and return to the house
where
my canine child stares out the window
into the night woods.

Workers at Mud Creek

My dog Belle and I circle the acre of green tomatoes.
This canine companion grabs a big tomato,
thinks it's a ball.

We have watched the plodding progress of this feat.
For three months, brown-skinned men
have worked this huge, humid, hot place
planting, staking, tying the round crop in place.
I glimpse a young boy working with them
from time to time.
I worry about him, bending his back, working the crop.
This hard green fruit is harvested now
to ripen between field and supermarket.

We leave and walk the creekside path
lined with lovely long, lavender Joe-Pye flowers.
I wonder,
can the workers see the flowers?

Roseless, the Grosbeak

She arrived flying through strange autumn winds.
Most would say, *a big sparrow?*
We knew she had a splendid mate
with a rose breast,
but he never appeared.
Her creamy browns did not
make our backyard colorful.
Yet she delighted us each noonday.
The lady had the appetite of an eagle,
gobbling sunflower seeds, berries, suet.
We took her for granted,
hoped she would stay all winter.
Two days ago something told her,
Fly South!
Roseless left the cold and wind
and did not even say good-bye.

Porch in Late August

Long ago
in late August
when summer was not over
and September not yet there,
aunts, cousins, children
spent time on the front porch,
a place to call out to neighbors
or to speak about porch plants
that bloom in the night.

Ladies wore bright cotton dresses.
Wicker furniture was made comfortable
with lumpy pillows.
Conversation was about gardens, politics,
or widowed Cousin Pauline, Cousin Blanche from Florida,
Aunt Lottie, who had departed this life.
Holly Springs, Dry Pond, Commerce, Athens, Gainesville
were mentioned.

Hot red crepe myrtle trees whispered among themselves.
They had heard it all before.

Photograph—Suite Mates in Berthas

Posed above the other college girls,
Elizabeth Hancock has high cheekbones
which the photographer has colored pink.
Her lace collar is a bertha from the Victorian era,
worn to cover the shoulders, dress up the outfit.

Lizzie, as she is called, is loved by everyone.
She will finish her training,
pass the Hall County teachers' test.
She will teach, marry James Bryan in December 1897.
They will have five children, Kathleen, Lucy, Ferd, May
and the youngest Frank, my father.
Lizzie gardens, teaches Sunday School.
She died of typhoid July 1907.

She was kind and good.
Everyone loved her,
students, family friends, black servants on the farm.
Now she lives on in stories
told to descendants
who never saw her.

My Dear Store

I remember Rich's department store in Atlanta.
Take the trolley from Oglethorpe University on Peachtree Road
to the end of the line.
Walk three blocks and enter this wonder palace.
From my five-year-old delight to middle age,
Rich's was a great star in my show.
The magical Christmas windows
had dolls telling Christmas stories.

My life always needed this store.
As a teenager, I asked for money, not gifts.
Then I hit the sales and always bought
a new white blouse and pencil skirt.
Every spring I bought a new swim suit
and a new Easter dress.

Shopping in the place was a mélange
of the ding, ding, ding, lights, clothes.
The day in 1960 when I received my first teaching
pay check from Dekalb County, Georgia,
I went to Rich's and applied for a credit card.
I soon bought my wedding dress,
a candlelight ivory satin tint.
The invitations were engraved at Dear Store.

When we built our house in 1969,
we found the book of house plans in the book department.
We bought all our son's clothes there until he married in 1989.
There I bought my mother-of-the-groom dress,
a really lovely pink.

In 2005 Rich's was gobbled up by a bigger company,
and Dear Store is no more.
The new one is not the same.

Beverly Bryan Russell   **87**

Artist and Child

Forty-six years ago.
Six Flags over Georgia, a theme park.
A young woman is doing chalk profiles for sale.
The Atlanta sun is very hot.
A three-year-old boy is presented to the artist.
She works quickly.
He hears people in line saying,
What a beautiful child, red hair, look at his eyes.
He knows he must sit still.
He does not know that
his mother will have the work framed
to hang in his bedroom
these many years,
a reminder of people, time and place.

Artist—Sue Holt   July, 1967
Child—Cameron Russell

The Magic Afghan

After long hard days I need rest.
I snuggle under a blanket
knitted with magic and love.
This coverlet was created
by loving hands
of one
who calmly sat and waited,
waited for doctors, dentists, lawyers.
Flying fingers worked soft wool,
green, green as moss.
The project grew bit by bit,
beauty in every stitch.
This gift, a labor of love,
comforts me.

The blanket noted was created by my sister,
the picture below is HB, another comfort in my life.

To Understand My Closets

To understand my closets,
you must open the doors
to get a quick glance.
I have jammed them for years.

To understand
you would have to pull everything out,
and put it neatly back,
minus the give-aways.

To understand why I don't put more
into the give-away pile—
My wedding dress and shoes are there.
My dress for our son's wedding is there.
I have quilts made by family members.
Thirty pocketbooks lie on a high shelf.
I love them.
There are coats of various lengths and colors.
Someday I may need them.

The problem is my family.
They think I should make a huge give-away pile.
Why it bothers them
is what I can't understand.

Your Place

A house is your place
to accumulate stuff,
a place to worry
about closets crammed to the rafters.
Eating, sleeping are important in a house.
You go there worn out at the end of each day.
It's a place to improve,
plan trips, rejoice when you return.
A house is a host to company.

Pets belong here to roam the rooms
and give them a used look.
People love each other here,
sometimes argue in loud voices.

The house is a fixer,
a stage to recover
from illness, grief, loss.
A house needs people.
Without them it becomes
stale, stationary, lonely.
A house may own the owner.
Even so, there is no place like it.

Letter to Myself

I will tell you what I know.
You must live in the present.
The future is full of sneaky surprises.
If you postpone joy, it may not be there
when you reach the long-awaited day.
If you live in the present,
you are safer because you can handle this day.
Don't fear tomorrow; let tomorrow wait until you get there.
An old song tells us, *Worry about tomorrow, tomorrow.*

Don't get too involved with toxic issues and people.
Pray for them instead.
Count your blessings.
Be thankful for friends and family.
Enjoy small things,
nature's beauties, smiles, the peace of the night.

The Edge of Dark

At twilight
roosting birds make settling-in sounds.
Cardinals cheep to each other.
Mothers call to children.
The edge makes all hurry.

Some months
cicadas tune up.
The frog gives a definite *ribit*.
Fortunate people may even see the foxfire.
Creatures seek cover
with nigh-cuts to each hole.
One dove coos.

Darkness arrives.

White Beauty

Good for you, beautiful pear trees.
Many say you split easily in ice storms.
What tree doesn't?
Go ahead,
flaunt your puffy white glory everywhere.
Raise winter sad spirits.
Cover up the gray landscape.
Override trash on roadsides we pass.
Gardeners think you are too large for lawns.
See yourself all over fields, forests,
any place.
Here, there, yon.

White.
White.
White.

Elizabeth B. Martinez

Always proud to claim having been the devoted Air Force wife, it was a far cry from my sprouting in Nova Scotia. Being raised in rural New England contributes, I believe, to my claiming a close relationship with the soil and the gut of reality. Thus, nature related subjects are often my themes of expression, as ants, birds and weather. Our travels, deeply etched in our memories, become our personal treasures. *The Excursion* sets its own timeline while *Journeys* is more recent.

Clearing Paths

Wielding the corn broom
the young maiden
deftly sweeps
the drifted snow
from the stoop steps
of the row house.

Not as easily
is she able to clear
the deep worries
clogging the
treacherous steps
of relationships
in her young life.

Form—ekphrasis: A written description of a work of art.
Sweeping Snow by Childe Hassam 1890

Ant Rant

My heart goes out
to all God's creatures,
hardly a one engages my wrath.
I try to live
in sweet acceptance
of the mouse
right up to the giraffe.

This season, though,
I take exception
to one that's causing my rant.
It's the thousands and thousands
of the teeniest, tiniest, craziest
scurrying ants

meeting each other
coming and going
from where to where
is the question.
I've put out the bait,
but they prefer crumbs
to satisfy their digestion.

I'm about to concede,
admit defeat.
They've gotten the best of me.

At my demise,
they'll file on over and
clean up what's left of me.

The Downy in Me

Observing the good-natured chaos
at the birdfeeder in my yard
brings memories
of our happy, vibrant family.

In years past, we gathered
for nourishment and
energized exchanges
at the oversized farm-kitchen table
with the side-benches,
where there was always
"room for one more!"

Oh, the jostling and joshing
that was part of the fare…
left us sated,
content and connected.

Now older, I live by myself,
find that I relate more
to the lonely Downy
who waits for the crowd to disperse,
then comes to dine
alone,
in the quiet.

Cold Spell

Uninvited, an old acquaintance
stopped by my place today.

With icy breath she greeted me—
no hint of length-of-stay.

Ill-prepared, I did my best,
proper protocol to master,

hoping that her visiting
would come to end much faster.

When asked, she said her time was short,
she was just passing through

wouldn't state how long she'd stay
nor what she'd come to do.

She finally left. I was relieved
and felt a whole lot better,

especially, as I lit my fire
and donned my thickest sweater.

Boeing Stratocruiser

Now, daily
I live with her picture
on the wall,
a portrait worthy
of her assets.
If share I must,
she is the least
of my angst.

We two
filled the major
hours of his life,
yet little did I know
of her. What I did overhear,
as the men in their
zippered flying suits talked,
was a most complimentary
trust of her qualities,
compliance during emergencies
and stability in long,
tedious airborne hours.

What a favored man,
my husband,
to have lived
and so loved
the two of us.

Journeys

It was a driving trip
not lightly planned
but long thought out,
a chance for one more short visit
with my older sister
at the nursing home,
while it was still feasible.

As the sun rose in Hendersonville
we started north to Pennsylvania.
Once in Virginia, Interstate 81 closely parallels
the Appalachian mountain range.

The miles flew by as my friend,
an Appalachian Trail hiker,
shared colorful memories of the walking peaks and paths.
What a special treat for me, to hear about the Trail
while viewing the breathtaking panorama.

A misty, intermittent rain moved in from the west
and claimed space from the morning sun.
The wipers were needed, off and on.
We were not prepared for what happened next…
A spot of color grew, took shape, just ahead on our left.
The movement never hesitated until
a perfect iridescent arch formed over our highway,
the outside arc a vibrant lavender.

Speechless, we drove toward it--
our own "'bow' in the sky."

Margaret Phelps
Jan 1923 – Dec 2011

The Excursion

My dad was never happy
when the promised time came around
to make the thirty-mile trip
from Littleton into Charlestown
so Mama could visit with her mother.
Oh, it wasn't that he didn't care for his in-laws,
he just was a man who was comfortable enough
with his days at the barn as he'd carved them out.
Any extra adventure, extra spice
was not needed in his mundane existence.

First, we had to see if the Model T Ford would start.
He would station me, standing, at the steering wheel,
the spark and throttle at the proper positions.
Then, straddling the front bumper, he would
give the crank a quick half turn.
It was my job, then, to quickly readjust the
spark and throttle to even off the rpm's.
I hated that job because the wrong timing
could result in an earsplitting BANG!
out the exhaust pipe. It seemed an extreme
responsibility assigned to the innocent.

Grandma lived on Eden Street near Bunker Hill.
Most of those adjoining streets were on steep inclines.
On approaching, Dad carefully drove to the top,
turned around and parked heading downward
in front of Grandma's door with the etched, oval glass.

The front tires were carefully turned into the curb,
in case the handbrake didn't hold.
The whole time we were there
—no matter how long the visit—
he sat in a chair he had drawn up to the window
to see that no big-city hoodlums
removed his tires.

Note: no hoodlums ever stole the tires!

Mama, in spite of Dad's disagreeable attitude,
went about enjoying the visit with her Mom,
marked by an occasional duet of raucous laughter
as they prepared a meal and kept an eye on
our activities exploring the small, fenced-in back yard
where we peeked through the knotholes in the fence,
spying on the neighborhood kids playing
hide and seek in the alley.

In the living room was the player piano.
Its paper rolls of magic holes, inserted properly,
made the operator on the bench a musical genius,
provided the vigorous foot pumping was not interrupted.
We had limited access to the piano.
Grandma also jealously guarded the old RCA Victrola.
Only she was allowed
to turn the wind-up arm and handle the records,
one of which was an Amos 'n' Andy skit about
two black crows on a telephone wire.

Grandpa sat chuckling
in his Morris chair with what I now know was
a brass spittoon next to the side arm.
He was a dear with a ready chuckle and had more patience
with grandkids than Grandma did—
even though he was not our real Grandpa.
I recall his oft-repeated admonition
to Grandma when we kids got noisy:
"Now, Lizzie,
(I was named Elizabeth, after her)
they're only children
having fun!"

Many times the visit came to an end when my Dad,
checking his pocket watch,
announced that he must get back in time
for the five-o'clock milking.
Reluctant, we piled back into the Model T,
(with four tires intact!),
and, clunking along over the street car tracks,
left the city for the pastoral scenes of Lexington and Concord.
Most of the trip home,
we three girls viewed on our knees,
playing games as we peered out the rear oval window,
watching the stone walled rural scenes disappear from view.

Current Members of the

Seasoned Poets of the Blue Ridge

Back: Laurabeth "Rusty" Breeding, Beverly Bryan Russell,
    Karen Heggen, Helen Palmer
Front: Elda Lepak, Gwyneth Owens Noble
Below: Elizabeth B. Martinez

Poets at play

Comments from the Poets

Helen Palmer

A transplanted Midwesterner, I fell in love with the mountains of Western North Carolina. After almost twenty-four years of retirement in Hendersonville, I feel that this is my home. I grew up in northeast Iowa, taught high school English in Iowa, and then for 31 years in Highland Park, Illinois. Retirement gave me a chance to pursue my interest in writing poetry; belonging for eighteen years to the Seasoned Poets group forced me to write almost weekly. In the early years I wrote free verse almost exclusively; lately I have returned to rhyming forms. Perhaps there is something satisfying about searching for the right rhyming word.

Gwyneth Owens Noble

From my "lofty perch", a euphemism for old age, I enjoy remembering the extensive traveling I had done before security checks at every point of a trip made traveling less attractive. I enjoy remembering children playing outside and hating to come in; young people graduating from college in four years unburdened by enormous debt. I celebrate people marrying for life. I welcome talking face to face with friends, hate to be involved in others' cell phone conversations. Though I gratefully send and receive e-mail from family and friends, I savor the long handwritten letters I still receive from two compatriots. Thoreau's admonition to "Simplify, simplify" speaks to me. In other words I've probably lived too long. Despite which I continue to enjoy the ever present challenges of life and the quiet beauty of nature. I give myself permission to comment freely on both.

Elda Lepak

Six years ago, I left Wisconsin and moved to North Carolina where I discovered and joined the Seasoned Poets of the Blue Ridge. My life opened up as I met weekly with this talented group of poets. We shared our poems and life histories, laughed and learned, and I grew in my understanding of what was missing in my life

My book *Sky Canvas* came out in 2010. Some of my poems appeared in two previous anthologies by our group, *Look Both Ways* and *A Long and Winding Road*. I've had poems published in *Free Verse, Verse Wisconsin, Wisconsin Poets' Calendar, The Main Street Rag, Song of the San Joaquin*, and the anthology *Empty Shoes: Poems on the Hungry and the Homeless*.

Karen Heggen

I have called Henderson County home since 1978. The Seasoned Poets and our ten anthologies have been my anchor for creative writing since 1994. My gardening now is limited to tending poems and family history. Nature and nurture, a sense of curiosity and the love of words spur me on. While today's pace of change seems swift as my own pace slows, it is remarkable to consider how short a time fifty years ago can seem. I follow the adage "to age gracefully, learn something new every day." Recently I am coming to terms with my first cell phone/smart phone and a Chromebook3 notebook computer.

In the coming year I plan to write both poems and articles about family history and put them online. YouTube is fine, but face to face still outranks Facebook to Facebook. May wit and wisdom be our best medicine.

Laurabeth "Rusty" Breeding

The descendants of my immigrant forebears are scattered across The United States and Canada. For this reason I grew up in a culture of letter writing. This familiarity with the pen gave me an outlet for my sense of rhythm, having inherited my father's soft, off-key voice, rather than my mother's, who was from a family of singers.

When I joined the Seasoned Poets of the Blue Ridge in 1994 I began to put regular effort into writing poetry and the effort has paid off with submissions in all our previous books. Many of my friends receive personalized poems in self-made birthday and other greeting cards. I think a little fun makes any season bright.

Beverly Bryan Russell

My voice has that Georgian born lilt, which finds its way into much of my writing. During my teaching career in North Carolina, my students and I created the literary magazine, *Socko*. In 1977 my short story "Helium Balloon" won the Appalachian Regional Writers Award. In retirement I joined the Seasoned Poets of the Blue Ridge and concentrated on poetry. My book *Telling Questions* was published in 2002, and *From the corner of My Eye* was published in 2008. Numerous poems have appeared in many of the Seasoned Poets anthologies. There is no end to new ideas for poems, though one must be ready when inspiration bubbles up.

Elizabeth B. Martinez

Early on, I was tempted by the printed world of self-expression although my paths led elsewhere. Later in life, youthful energies harnessed, offspring launched, retirement years in view, I had the good fortune to happen onto a writing group made up of others with like ambitions. The Seasoned Poets of the Blue Ridge have been crucial angels in this endeavor. I shall be forever grateful for their love and support.

Anthologies: Seasoned Poets of the Blue Ridge

Beyond Flower Gardens   1994
Apple Country: Hendersonville Poems   1996
Standing On Our Words   1997
Swimming in Stars   1998
The Taste of Waking   2000
Just to the Right of the Moon   2002
Time Keepers   2006
Look Both Ways   2009
A Long and Winding Road   2011

Additional Titles by the Seasoned Poets

Hazel Herndon Fryer

One Brash Mockingbird   1955
A Handful of Sand   1997
If I Were a Tree   1999
Paper Trail   2001
The Gift of Words   2002

Elda Lepak

Sky Canvas   2010

Gwyneth Owens Noble

The Ladder Holder   1996
A Shadowy Music   1999
Just a Shadow of Myself   2004
In Love with Shadows   2008

Helen Palmer
> *Jigsaw Puzzle   1997*
> *Spilled out of the Jar of Memory   2003*

Edith Pedersen
> *Where the Wild Grasses Grow   1997*

Beverly Bryan Russell
> *Telling Questions   2002*
> *From the Corner of My Eye   2008*

Francis Miner Schneider
> *Haying Time   1997*